Stay Safe Online

Level 6 – Orange

Helpful Hints for Reading at Home

The graphemes (written letters) and phonemes (units of sound) used throughout this series are aligned with Letters and Sounds. This offers a consistent approach to learning whether reading at home or in the classroom.

HERE IS A LIST OF PHONEMES FOR THIS PHASE OF LEARNING. AN EXAMPLE OF THE PRONUNCIATION CAN BE FOUND IN BRACKETS.

Phase 5			
ay (day)	ou (out)	ie (tie)	ea (eat)
oy (boy)	ir (girl)	ue (blue)	aw (saw)
wh (when)	ph (photo)	ew (new)	oe (toe)
au (Paul)	a_e (make)	e_e (these)	i_e (like)
o_e (home)	u_e (rule, cube)		

Phase 5 Alternative Pronunciations of Graphemes			
a (hat, what)	e (bed, she)	i (fin, find)	o (hot, so, other)
u (but, unit)	c (cat, cent)	g (got, giant)	ow (cow, blow)
ie (tied, field)	ea (eat, bread)	er (farmer, herb)	ch (chin, school, chef)
y (yes, by, very)	ou (out, shoulder, could, you)		

HERE ARE SOME WORDS WHICH YOUR CHILD MAY FIND TRICKY.

Phase 5 Tricky Words			
oh	their	people	Mr
Mrs	looked	called	asked
could			

TOP TIPS FOR HELPING YOUR CHILD TO READ:

- Allow children time to break down unfamiliar words into units of sound and then encourage children to string these sounds together to create the word.

- Encourage your child to point out any focus phonics when they are used.

- Read through the book more than once to grow confidence.

- Ask simple questions about the text to assess understanding.

- Encourage children to use illustrations as prompts.

This book focuses on the phonemes /a_e/, /ay/ and /i_e/ and is an orange level 6 book band.

Can you work out which of these pictures have names with i_e in them?

Answers: nine, smile, bike, kite, wires

When we are on the internet, we say that we are online. It is important that we stay safe when we are online.

Lots of people like the internet. There is lots to see and do. People across the planet can all be online at the same time.

We can play games with lots of people online. We can dive into a car chase or a tennis match.

We can chat with lots of people too. We can invite mates to chat on lots of internet websites.

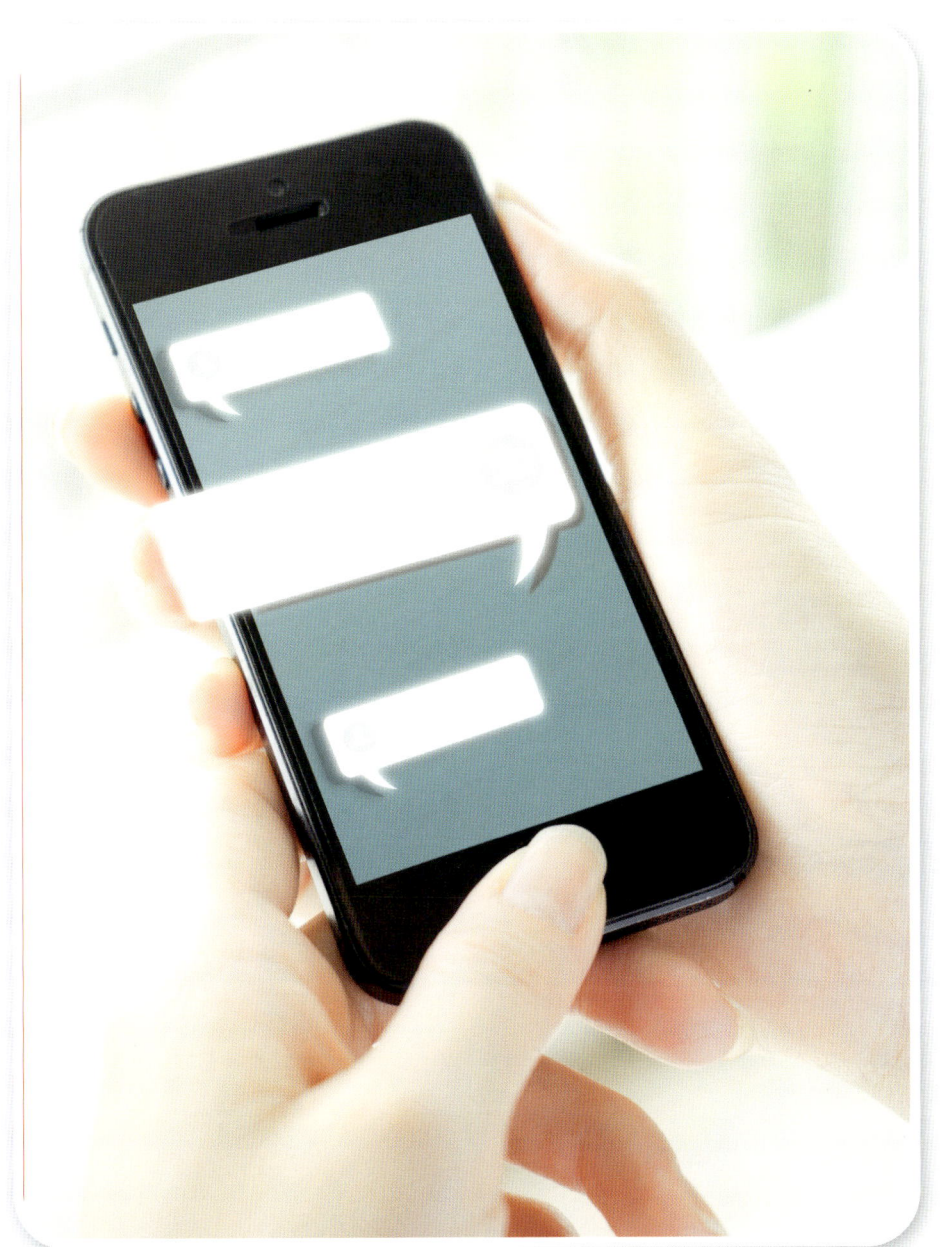

But we must keep safe when we are online so that we do not sway into problems.

Can you think of problems you may get into online?

Some people do not behave in the same way when they are online. They may not be the same as they are in real life.

Some people may say mean things when they are online. It is important to chat with an adult if someone upsets you.

Some websites are not made for kids. Speak to an adult to ask which websites you can visit, so they can make sure things are safe.

We can chat with lots of people online. But not all people on the internet are the same person they say they are.

Never agree to meet people you chat with online. Always make sure you speak to an adult that you trust if someone asks to meet you.

You do need to be safe online, but you do not need to hide away from the internet.

Lots of websites are good and filled with fun things to make us smile. We can all enjoy the internet, as long as we stay safe.

©2021 **BookLife Publishing Ltd.**
King's Lynn, Norfolk PE30 4LS

ISBN 978-1-83927-905-8

All rights reserved. Printed in England.
A catalogue record for this book is available
from the British Library.

Stay Safe Online
Written by William Anthony
Designed by Amy Li

An Introduction to BookLife Readers...

Our Readers have been specifically created in line with the London Institute of Education's approach to book banding and are phonetically decodable and ordered to support each phase of the Letters and Sounds document.

Each book has been created to provide the best possible reading and learning experience. Our aim is to share our love of books with children, providing both emerging readers and prolific page-turners with beautiful books that are guaranteed to provoke interest and learning, regardless of ability.

BOOK BAND GRADED using the Institute of Education's approach to levelling.

PHONETICALLY DECODABLE supporting each phase of Letters and Sounds.

EXERCISES AND QUESTIONS to offer reinforcement and to ascertain comprehension.

CLEAR DESIGN to inspire and provoke engagement, providing the reader with clear visual representations of each non-fiction topic.

AUTHOR INSIGHT:
WILLIAM ANTHONY

Despite his young age, William Anthony's involvement with children's education is quite extensive. He has written over 60 titles with BookLife Publishing so far, across a wide range of subjects. William graduated from Cardiff University with a 1st Class BA (Hons) in Journalism, Media and Culture, creating an app and a TV series, among other things, during his time there.

William Anthony has also produced work for the Prince's Trust, a charity created by HRH The Prince of Wales that helps young people with their professional future. He has created animated videos for a children's education company that works closely with the charity.

PHASE 5
/a_e/ay/
/i_e/

This book focuses on the phonemes /a_e/, /ay/ and /i_e/ and is an orange level 6 book band.

Image Credits Images are courtesy of Shutterstock.com. With thanks to Getty Images, Thinkstock Photo and iStockphoto.
Cover – Prophotoo, Lenka Horavova, 24Novembers, Sidorova Vera, p2–3 – CapturePB, FabrikaSimf, Kateryna998, Mega Pixel, Mindscape, Pixel-Shot, Regreto, vector. p4–5 – ESB Professional, CreativeAngela, p6–7 – Martin Vorel, PHOTOBUAY, p8–9 – LightField Studios, Richy99, p10–11 – Milano Art, Monkey Business Images, Rawpixel.com, p12–13 – Marcos Mesa Sam Wordley, michaeljung, p14–15 – fizkes, KK Tan.